WALLACE STEGNER

JOANNE MATTERN

ABDO Publishing Company

visit us at
www.abdopublishing.com

Printed in the United States of America, North Mankato, Minnesota.
112013
012014

♻ PRINTED ON RECYCLED PAPER

Cover Photo: Glow Images, Corbis
Interior Photos: Alamy p. 1; AP Images pp. 11, 13, 15, 19, 20, 25, 27; Corbis p. 23; Getty Images pp. 5, 8–9, 21; iStockphoto p. 17; MELVILLE B. GROSVENOR / National Geographic Creative p. 22; Thinkstock p. 7

Editors: Rochelle Baltzer, Megan M. Gunderson, Bridget O'Brien
Art Direction: Neil Klinepier

Library of Congress Control Number: 2013951996

Cataloging-in-Publication Data

Mattern, Joanne.
 Wallace Stegner / Joanne Mattern.
  p. cm. -- (Conservationists)
Includes bibliographical references and index.
ISBN 978-1-62403-097-0
1. Stegner, Wallace, 1909-1993--Juvenile literature. 2. Authors, American--20th century--Biography--Juvenile literature. 3. Conservationists--United States--Biography--Juvenile literature. 4. Historians--United States--Biography--Juvenile literature. 1. Title.
333.72092--dc23
[B]

2013951996

CONTENTS

THE WEST

Wallace Stegner was born in the middle of the United States. Over 84 years, he lived in the East, in the West, and up into Canada.

Stegner found beauty wherever he lived, but his heart was in the West. Through his writings and conservation work, he became one of the most important voices calling for the preservation of Western lands.

Wallace Earle Stegner was born on a farm in Lake Mills, Iowa, on February 18, 1909. He had an older brother named Cecil.

Wallace's parents were George H. and Hilda Paulson Stegner. They were Scandinavian **immigrants**. Hilda's main job was to care for the children. George had many different jobs. He was always looking for a way to strike it rich. He moved the family from place to place in search of success.

Wallace Stegner

WANDERING

George moved his family many times while Wallace was growing up. Before age 12, Wallace lived in Iowa, North Dakota, Washington, Canada, and Montana.

In Washington, the family was so poor that the boys spent time in an **orphanage**. They lived there until their mother could make enough money to get them out again. Then, they spent several months in Iowa with Hilda's father.

George had already moved to Eastend, Saskatchewan, in Canada. The rest of the family joined him there in 1914. In Canada, George worked on a farm during the summer. During the winter, he found jobs in town.

Wallace helped his father with farmwork. He also attended school. Saskatchewan has large stretches of prairies. And Wallace spent hours exploring them.

Wallace traveled to Eastend by horse-drawn wagon.

Books & Sports

In spring 1920, the Stegner family moved to Great Falls, Montana. Then in 1921, they settled in Salt Lake City, Utah. Wallace spent the next ten years there.

In Salt Lake City, Wallace attended public school. He did well with his studies, but he felt like an outsider and was often bullied. Things were not much better at home. Wallace's father was much closer with Cecil, who was a good athlete.

Wallace found his own ways to be happy. He checked out four to six books a week from the library. Wallace also was active in the Boy Scouts. He enjoyed their outdoor programs and found a feeling of community.

Wallace graduated from high school in 1926, when he was 16 years old. During his final year, Wallace had grown six inches (15 cm) and gained muscle. For the first time, he was able to compete successfully in sports. Twice, Wallace's mother saw him intently watching people playing tennis. She bought him a racket, and he began a lifelong love of the game.

Even in Salt Lake City, Wallace's family didn't stop moving. There, they lived in nearly a dozen different homes.

COLLEGE LIFE

After high school, it was time for Stegner to go to college and find his place in the world. He began his higher education at the University of Utah in Salt Lake City. Stegner had to work to pay his way through school. But, he still found time to play on the tennis team and have many friends. He also spent time hunting, fishing, and exploring the outdoors.

In 1930, Stegner graduated from the University of Utah with a degree in English. He received a graduate teaching **fellowship** at the University of Iowa. So, he moved to Iowa City to continue attending school.

The next few years were busy. Stegner earned his master's degree from Iowa in 1932. But that wasn't the end of Stegner's schooling. He continued on toward a PhD.

Stegner also suffered two painful family losses during his school years. In 1930, his brother died of **pneumonia**. His mother died of **cancer** just three years later.

Stegner's parents ended their formal education before finishing sixth grade. Stegner went on to earn a PhD and become a lifelong teacher.

A New Family

     To earn his PhD, Stegner continued his studies at the University of Iowa. While in school, he began his lifelong career in teaching. He traveled back and forth to Augustana College in Rock Island, Illinois. There, he taught English for a time.

     In Iowa, Stegner met a fellow graduate student named Mary Stuart Page. The two fell in love and married on September 1, 1934. They would be married for 59 years. In 1937, the couple had their only child. They named their son Stuart Page. Page grew up to be an author and teacher like his father.

     The Stegners moved back to Salt Lake City in 1934. There, Stegner taught at the University of Utah. He officially earned his PhD the following year. Then in 1937, Stegner received news that would change his life forever.

Mary, Page, and Wallace Stegner in 1950

WINNING WORDS

In 1936, Stegner had entered a short novel called *Remembering Laughter* into a contest. Just a few days before his son's birth, Stegner received wonderful news. He had won the contest!

Stegner was awarded $2,500, which was a lot of money in 1937. It was more than Stegner could make teaching in a year! And, the book sold well.

Stegner realized that he could be both a teacher and a writer. To do so, he kept to a specific schedule. In the morning, he wrote for three or four hours. During the afternoon, he taught classes. After class, Stegner exercised or worked outside. At night, Stegner read, corrected papers, prepared for class, and entertained friends.

Stegner was an excellent writer. But as a young man, he didn't know writing could be a career.

TEACHING LIFE

Stegner and his family moved many times over the next few years as he took different jobs. He taught at the University of Wisconsin–Madison from 1937 to 1939. From 1939 to 1945, he worked at Harvard University in Cambridge, Massachusetts. There, he taught **composition**.

Beginning in 1938, Stegner joined the Bread Loaf Writers' Conference in Vermont. There he met famous poet Robert Frost, who was a fellow instructor. Frost and Stegner became good friends.

After **World War II**, Stegner became an English professor at Stanford University in California. He began teaching there in 1945 and would continue for about 25 years.

Stegner's most important role at Stanford was directing the school's creative writing program. Several of Stegner's students went on to become famous writers. They included Old West novelist Larry McMurtry and **environmentalist** and novelist Edward Abbey.

Stegner loved living in the West. He began writing about the beauty of this part of the nation. He was especially concerned with its preservation. Soon, he would become one of the country's most outspoken conservationists.

Stanford University

FUN FACT:

The success of Remembering Laughter *helped Stegner get his job at Harvard.*

DINOSAUR

During the 1950s, Stegner found out that part of Dinosaur National Monument was in danger. This wilderness area is on the border between Utah and Colorado. It contains ancient dinosaur fossils and **petroglyphs**. It also features beautiful canyons, rivers, and wildlife.

Now the US government wanted to build a dam in Echo Park, an area of the monument. This would flood a large area of the land. Conservationists were horrified. They said that if land in a national monument was not safe from development, then none of America's treasured places were safe.

In 1955, Stegner edited a book called *This is Dinosaur: Echo Park Country and Its Magic Rivers*. The book's essays and photos made readers aware of the area's beauty. It was sent to every member of the US Congress. The public also voiced their concerns. Congress listened, and it did not allow the dam in Echo Park.

Dinosaur National Monument in the 1950s. This area would have been flooded by the Echo Park dam Stegner worked to stop.

THE WILDERNESS

After Dinosaur, Stegner stayed involved in the conservation movement. In 1960, he wrote what became known as the Wilderness Letter. It called for federal protection of wild places. He said they were vital for all people, and they should be protected.

The Wilderness Letter became an important part of the movement to save America's wilderness. Secretary of the Interior Stewart Udall read it at a convention asking the government to preserve more wild places.

Secretary of the Interior Stewart Udall served under presidents John F. Kennedy and Lyndon B. Johnson.

CONSERVATION ALERT!

Since the Wilderness Act came into law, Congress has protected more than 57 million acres (23 million ha) of land in Alaska alone.

In 1964, the government passed the Wilderness Act. This law created the National Wilderness Preservation System. Since the act came into law, Congress has protected more than 106 million acres (43 million ha) of wild American land.

Stegner's Wilderness Letter became a very important document for environmentalists. It has been quoted endlessly and even used on posters around the world.

NATURE WORK

Stegner (far right) *with Secretary Udall* (second from left) *and members of the National Parks Advisory Board in Glacier Bay National Monument, Alaska*

In 1961, Secretary Udall asked Stegner to be his assistant. Then in 1962, he appointed Stegner to the National Park Service Advisory Board. Stegner served for three years and was chairman of the board in his last year. The board advises the secretary of the interior and the director of the National Park Service (NPS) about NPS programs, proposed sites, and other matters.

Stegner participated in the Sierra Club for more than 40 years.

These responsibilities allowed Stegner to speak out for preservation. Stegner also educated people through his writing. He published many magazine articles about **environmental** issues. He was dedicated to sharing the beauty of the natural world. Stegner also wanted to save places near his home in California. He helped found the Committee for the Green Foothills in San Mateo and Santa Clara counties in 1960. This organization works to preserve open spaces in California. Stegner also worked with major national organizations including the Sierra Club and the Wilderness Society.

FUN FACT:

The Sierra Club was founded by conservationist John Muir in 1892. The organization works to protect the environment in the United States and Canada.

HONORED AUTHOR

Stegner continued to write and teach throughout the 1960s. In 1971, he retired from Stanford University. But he kept on writing.

Stegner's novel *Angle of Repose* won the **Pulitzer Prize** for fiction in 1972. This is one of the highest honors any writer can achieve. Then in 1977, Stegner won the **National Book Award** for his novel *The Spectator Bird*.

Stegner didn't accept every award he was offered. In 1992, a government agency called the National Endowment for the Arts (NEA) wanted to give him the National Medal for the Arts. Stegner turned down the award. He said he didn't like the political pressure the government had put on the NEA. He felt they were not completely free to support the arts.

Stegner based some of his stories on events and people in his own life.

LIFE WELL LIVED

In March 1993, the Stegners traveled to Santa Fe, New Mexico, for an awards ceremony. While there, they were involved in a serious car accident. Mary was unhurt, but Stegner had serious injuries. He died two weeks later, on April 13. His ashes were scattered near his summer home in Vermont.

Wallace Stegner left behind a lifetime of hard work and creativity. His novels are still popular today. And, his work shows people the beauty of the natural world.

Stegner's conservation work made a difference. He helped show the US government how important it is to protect wild places. During his life, Stegner lived in many different places in the United States and Canada. He found beauty worth saving everywhere he went.

Stegner was survived by his wife, son, daughter-in-law, and three grandchildren.

TIMELINE

1909 ● Wallace Earle Stegner was born on February 18 in Lake Mills, Iowa.

1921 ● The Stegner family settled in Salt Lake City, Utah.

1926 ● Stegner graduated from high school at age 16.

1930 ● Stegner graduated from the University of Utah in Salt Lake City with a degree in English; his brother died of pneumonia.

1932 ● Stegner earned a master's degree from the University of Iowa in Iowa City.

1933 ● Stegner's mother died of cancer.

1934 ● On September 1, Stegner married Mary Stuart Page; the Stegners moved to Salt Lake City.

1935 ● Stegner earned a PhD from the University of Iowa.

1937 ● Stegner's short novel *Remembering Laughter* won a contest and was published; his son Stuart Page was born.

1938 ● Stegner joined the Bread Loaf Writers' Conference in Vermont.

1945 ●	Stegner began teaching at Stanford University in California.
1955 ●	Stegner edited *This is Dinosaur: Echo Park Country and Its Magic Rivers.*
1960 ●	Stegner wrote the Wilderness Letter; he helped found the Committee for the Green Foothills.
1961 ●	Stegner became assistant to Secretary of the Interior Stewart Udall.
1962 ●	Udall appointed Stegner to the National Park Service Advisory Board.
1964 ●	The Wilderness Act passed.
1972 ●	*Angle of Repose* was awarded the Pulitzer Prize.
1977 ●	*The Spectator Bird* won the National Book Award.
1992 ●	Stegner turned down the National Medal for the Arts.
1993 ●	Stegner died on April 13 in Santa Fe, New Mexico.

"Something will have gone out of us as a people if we ever let the remaining wilderness be destroyed." —Wallace Stegner

29

GLOSSARY

cancer - any of a group of often deadly diseases marked by harmful changes in the normal growth of cells. Cancer can spread and destroy healthy tissues and organs.

composition - a type of writing, especially referring to brief essays.

environmentalist - a person concerned with problems of the environment. The environment is all the surroundings that affect the growth and well-being of a living thing.

fellowship - the position of a person appointed for advanced study or research.

immigrant - a person who enters another country to live.

National Book Award - an annual award given to a book written by an American author and produced by an American publisher.

orphanage - a place for the care of children, usually those with no parents.

petroglyph (PEH-truh-glihf) - a usually prehistoric drawing carved in rock.

pneumonia (nuh-MOH-nyuh) - a disease that affects the lungs. It may cause fever, coughing, or difficulty breathing.

Pulitzer Prize - one of several annual awards established by journalist Joseph Pulitzer. The awards honor accomplishments in journalism, literature, drama, and music.

World War II - from 1939 to 1945, fought in Europe, Asia, and Africa.

WEB SITES

To learn more about Wallace Stegner, visit ABDO Publishing Company online. Web sites about Wallace Stegner are featured on our Book Links page. These links are routinely monitored and updated to provide the most current information available. **www.abdopublishing.com**

INDEX